alto
saxophone

Now you c
alto saxoph
specially rec

# NUMBER ONE HITS

# TAKE THE LEAD

## alto saxophone

IMP
International MUSIC Publications

International Music Publications Limited
Griffin House 161 Hammersmith Road London W6 8BS England

Series Editor: Sadie Cook

Editorial, production and recording: Artemis Music Limited
Design and production: Space DPS Limited

Published 2000

**International MUSIC Publications**

© International Music Publications Limited
Griffin House 161 Hammersmith Road London W6 8BS England

International Music Publications Limited

**England:** Griffin House
161 Hammersmith Road
London W6 8BS

**Germany:** Marstallstr. 8
D-80539 München

**Denmark:** Danmusik
Vognmagergade 7
DK1120 Copenhagen K

**Italy:** Nuova Carisch Srl
Via Campania 12
20098 San Giuliano Milanese
Milano

**Spain:** Nueva Carisch España
Magallanes 25
28015 Madrid

**France:** Carisch Musicom
25 Rue d'Hauteville
75010 Paris

**WARNER BROS. PUBLICATIONS U.S. INC.**

**USA:** 15800 N.W. 48th Avenue
Miami, Florida 33014

**Australia:** 3 Talavera Road
North Ryde
New South Wales 2113

**Scandinavia:** P.O. Box 533
Vendevägen 85 B
S-182 15 Danderyd
Sweden

**alto saxophone**

# TAKE THE LEAD

## In the Book...

Believe . . . . . . . . . . . . . . . . . . . . . . . . . . 6

Careless Whisper . . . . . . . . . . . . . . . . . . 12

Dancing Queen . . . . . . . . . . . . . . . . . . 14

Flying Without Wings . . . . . . . . . . . . . . . 16

I Will Always Love You . . . . . . . . . . . . . 18

Livin' La Vida Loca . . . . . . . . . . . . . . . 20

When You Say Nothing At All . . . . . . 9

You Needed Me . . . . . . . . . . . . . . . . . 22

# On the CD...

Track **1**    Tuning Tones (A Concert)

## Believe
Track **2**    Full version
Track **3**    Backing track

## When You Say Nothing At All
Track **4**    Full version
Track **5**    Backing track

## Careless Whisper
Track **6**    Full version
Track **7**    Backing track

## Dancing Queen
Track **8**    Full version
Track **9**    Backing track

## Flying Without Wings
Track **10**    Full version
Track **11**    Backing track

## I Will Always Love You
Track **12**    Full version
Track **13**    Backing track

## Livin' La Vida Loca
Track **14**    Full version
Track **15**    Backing track

## You Needed Me
Track **16**    Full version
Track **17**    Backing track

Demonstration    Backing

# Believe

Words and Music by
Brian Higgins, Stuart McLennan, Paul Barry,
Stephen Torch, Matt Gray and Tim Powell

**Brightly**

Demonstration

Backing

# When You Say Nothing At All

Words and Music by
Paul Overstreet and Don Schlitz

Demonstration

Backing

# Careless Whisper

Words and Music by
George Michael and Andrew Ridgeley

**Rather Slow**

Demonstration    Backing

# Dancing Queen

Words and Music by Benny Andersson,
Stig Anderson and Björn Ulvaeus

Demonstration

Backing

# Flying Without Wings

Words and Music by
Steve Mac and Wayne Hector

Demonstration

Backing

# I Will Always Love You

Words and Music by
Dolly Parton

# Livin' La Vida Loca

Words and Music by
Robi Rosa and Desmond Child

Demonstration  Backing

# You Needed Me

Words and Music by
Randy Goodrum

**Gently**

# You can be the featured soloist with
# TAKE THE LEAD

Now you can be the feature clarinet soloist on eight specially recorded arrangements

**TAKE THE LEAD**

**clarinet**

**FEATURES**
* Full backings to play along with
* Full demonstration tracks to help you learn the songs
* Carefully selected and edited arrangements
* Chord symbols in concert pitch

**MOVIE HITS**

## Collect these titles, each with demonstration and full backing tracks on CD

### 90s Hits

The Air That I Breathe (Simply Red)
Angels (Robbie Williams)
How Do I Live (LeAnn Rimes)
I Don't Want To Miss A Thing (Aerosmith)
I'll Be There For You (The Rembrandts)
My Heart Will Go On (Celine Dion)
Something About The Way
You Look Tonight (Elton John)
Frozen (Madonna)

Order ref: 6725A – Flute
Order ref: 6726A – Clarinet
Order ref: 6727A – Alto Saxophone
Order ref: 6728A – Violin

### Movie Hits

Because You Loved Me (Up Close And Personal)
Blue Monday (The Wedding Singer)
(Everything I Do)
I Do It For You (Robin Hood: Prince Of Thieves)
I Don't Want To Miss A Thing (Armageddon)
I Will Always Love You (The Bodyguard)
Star Wars (Main Title) (Star Wars)
The Wind Beneath My Wings (Beaches)
You Can Leave Your Hat On (The Full Monty)

Order ref: 6908A – Flute
Order ref: 6909A – Clarinet
Order ref: 6910A – Alto Saxophone
Order ref: 6911A –Tenor Saxophone
Order ref: 6912A – Violin

### TV Themes

Coronation Street
I'll Be There For You (theme from *Friends*)
Match Of The Day
(Meet) The Flintstones
Men Behaving Badly
Peak Practice
The Simpsons
The X-Files

Order ref: 7003A – Flute
Order ref: 7004A – Clarinet
Order ref: 7005A – Alto Saxophone
Order ref: 7006A – Violin

### Christmas Song

The Christmas Song
(Chestnuts Roasting On An Open F
Frosty The Snowman
Have Yourself A Merry Little Christ
Little Donkey
Rudolph The Red-Nosed Reinde
Santa Claus Is Comin' To Town
Sleigh Ride
Winter Wonderland

Order ref: 7022A – Flute
Order ref: 7023A – Clarinet
Order ref: 7024A – Alto Saxophone
Order ref: 7025A – Violin
Order ref: 7026A – Piano
Order ref: 7027A – Drums

### The Blues Brothers

She Caught The Katy And Left Me A Mule To Ride
Gimme Some Lovin'
Shake A Tail Feather
Everybody Needs Somebody To Love
The Old Landmark
Think
Minnie The Moocher
Sweet Home Chicago

Order ref: 7079A - Flute
Order ref: 7080A - Clarinet
Order ref: 7081A - Alto Saxophone
Order ref: 7082A - Tenor Saxophone
Order ref: 7083A - Trumpet
Order ref: 7084A - Violin

### Latin

Bailamos
Cherry Pink And
Apple Blossom White
Guantanamera
La Bamba
La Isla Bonita
Livin' La Vida Loca
Oye Mi Canto (Hear My Voice)
Soul Limbo

Order ref: 7259A - Flute
Order ref: 7260A - Clarinet
Order ref: 7261A - Alto Saxophone
Order ref: 7364A - Piano
Order ref: 7262A - Trumpet
Order ref: 7263A - Violin

### Jazz

Birdland
Desafinado
Don't Get Around Much Anymore
Fascinating Rhythm
Misty
My Funny Valentine
One O'Clock Jump
Summertime

Order ref: 7124A - Flute
Order ref: 7173A - Clarinet
Order ref: 7174A - Alto Saxophone
Order ref: 7175A - Tenor Saxophone
Order ref: 7179A - Drums
Order ref: 7178A - Piano
Order ref: 7176A - Trumpet
Order ref: 7177A - Violin

### Swing

Chattanooga Choo Choo
Choo Choo Ch'Boogie
I've Got A Gal In Kalamazoo
In The Mood
It Don't Mean A Thing
(If It Ain't Got That Swing)
Jersey Bounce
Pennsylvania 6-5000
A String Of Pearls

Order ref: 7235A - Flute
Order ref: 7236A - Clarinet
Order ref: 7237A - Alto Saxophone
Order ref: 7238A - Tenor Saxophone
Order ref: 7239A - Trumpet
Order ref: 7240A - Violin